AF270671

BADWATER 135

ANTHONY K. HEWSON

SportsZone

An Imprint of Abdo Publishing
abdobooks.com

abdobooks.com

Published by Abdo Publishing, a division of ABDO, PO Box 398166, Minneapolis, Minnesota 55439. Copyright © 2024 by Abdo Consulting Group, Inc. International copyrights reserved in all countries. No part of this book may be reproduced in any form without written permission from the publisher. SportsZone™ is a trademark and logo of Abdo Publishing.

Printed in the United States of America, North Mankato, Minnesota.
102023
012024

Cover Photo: David McNew/Getty Images News/Getty Images
Interior Photos: Ezra Shaw/Getty Images Sport/Getty Images, 4–5, 13, 16, 29; Red Line Editorial, 6; David McNew/Getty Images News/Getty Images, 9, 19, 20, 26; Robyn Beck/AFP/Getty Images, 10–11, 15; Toni L. Sandys/Washington Post/Getty Images, 22–23; Chris Carlson/AP Images, 24–25

Editor: Steph Giedd
Series Designer: Cynthia Della-Rovere

Library of Congress Control Number: 2023939864

Publisher's Cataloging-in-Publication Data

Names: Hewson, Anthony K., author.
Title: Badwater 135 / by Anthony K. Hewson
Other title: Badwater One Hundred Thirty-Five
Description: Minneapolis, Minnesota: Abdo Publishing, 2024 | Series: Extreme sports events | Includes online resources and index.
Identifiers: ISBN 9781098292331 (lib. bdg.) | ISBN 9798384910275 (ebook)
Subjects: LCSH: Extreme sports--Juvenile literature. | Action sports (Extreme sports)--Juvenile literature. | Ultra-marathon running--Juvenile literature. | Running races--Juvenile literature. | Deserts--Juvenile literature. | Mountains--Juvenile literature.
Classification: DDC 796.046--dc23

TABLE OF CONTENTS

CHAPTER 1

The World's Toughest Footrace 4

CHAPTER 2

Train to Reign 10

CHAPTER 3

Pounding the Pavement 18

CHAPTER 4

The Greatest Reward 24

Glossary 30
More Information 31
Online Resources 31
Index 32
About the Author 32

THE WORLD'S TOUGHEST FOOTRACE

n the pitch-dark California desert, a gunshot rings out. The 2018 Badwater 135—commonly known as "the World's Toughest Footrace"—is underway. Starting at night is by design. The race begins in one of the hottest places on Earth—Death Valley, California.

Pamela Chapman-Markle's heart races as she takes off from the starting line, even though she is as experienced in the Badwater as anyone. By the time of the 2018 race, Pam had set the women's 60-plus record three years in a row. The 63-year-old wants to beat the record again. But experience matters only so much.

Five miles (8 km) into her journey, the dry desert air is burning her throat and lungs.

The Badwater 135 starts at night due to the extreme daytime temperatures in Death Valley.

DEATH VALLEY NATIONAL PARK

Death Valley National Park is the "hottest, driest, and lowest national park" in terms of elevation. It experiences constant droughts and record temperatures in the summer. Pam wears a light on her belt that serves as her only guidance down the roadway. She is hundreds of miles away from the bright lights of Las Vegas, the closest city to Death Valley National Park. Pam runs 42 miles (67.6 km) in solitude and darkness before dawn.

As Pam begins to tire, she gets assistance from her crew of supporters, who drive in a car alongside her. They give her ice to chew on and to dump under her clothes. Daylight brings brutal temperatures of nearly 130 degrees Fahrenheit (54°C). The year before, Pam went through four pairs of shoes. The soles of the first three melted in the heat.

Only a few people are physically capable of completing such a run. And even those who can do it train for months to physically survive the challenge. It's called the world's toughest footrace for a reason.

FROM LOW TO HIGH

The Badwater 135 is known as an ultramarathon. Officially speaking, an ultramarathon is any footrace longer than a traditional marathon distance of 26.2 miles (42.2 km). But not all these races are created equal. The Badwater is more than five times the length of a traditional marathon. It also subjects racers to extreme temperatures and elevation changes.

Adventurous athletes have been attempting runs across similar routes since the 1960s. But the Badwater first became an official race in 1987. Only five participants took part that year. Today, entries are capped at 100. Anywhere from 20 to 40 percent of participants, who are the best ultramarathoners in the world, fail to finish.

The race gets its name from Badwater Basin, where the starting line is in Death Valley. At 280 feet (85 m) below sea level, it is the lowest point in North America. The ending point of the race is on Mount Whitney, the highest mountain in the contiguous United States, 85 miles (137 km) away. But the racers don't get to travel those 85 miles in a straight line. The Badwater racecourse is instead a winding, brutal 135-mile (217-km) path through some of the most extreme temperatures on Earth. The distance is where the Badwater 135 gets the other half of its name.

One of the first landmarks racers pass through is Furnace Creek, California. Despite having "creek" in its name, it is one of the driest places in North America. But the location does indeed feel like a furnace. In 1913 Furnace Creek had a recorded temperature of 134 degrees Fahrenheit (57°C). That set a world record.

Runners in the Badwater 135 don't reach the summit of Mount Whitney. The race concludes at the start of the trail up to the peak, which is still 8,300 feet (2,530 m) above the desert basin. The final stretch is perhaps the toughest,

Runners have support crews who help keep them cool during the race.

as runners endure a 4,600-foot (1,402-m) climb over the final 13 miles (20.9 km) to the finish line.

The challenge of the Badwater draws participants from all over the world. In 2022 runners came from 25 countries. They ranged in age from 31 to 71. All Badwater runners come to test themselves in one of the most prestigious extreme sporting events on Earth.

CHAPTER 2

TRAIN TO REIGN

It is the challenge of the Badwater 135 that attracts the best endurance athletes in the world. It is also because of that challenge that not just anyone can show up and run the race. The Badwater is an invitational—racers have to apply for entry. And there are only 100 spots available.

There are a few reasons the Badwater 135 is an invitational race. One is simply numbers—thousands of people apply each year. The race, which is run mostly on public roads, could get overcrowded. But the primary reason is for the safety of the athletes. Allowing unprepared runners to take part could lead to serious injury or death.

Arthur Webb, *far right,* has completed the race 14 times.

To be accepted, athletes need to demonstrate their history of success in similar races. Even previously finishing a Badwater 135 isn't enough to qualify. Previous finishers also need to have completed another ultramarathon in the year prior to applying.

The bar is even higher for runners who have never finished the Badwater 135. They need to have finished four other races of 100 miles (161 km) or more to qualify for application. They also need at least three years of history participating in ultramarathons.

Even so, just meeting one of these standards does not guarantee entry. Of the 100 spots available, the entry committee tries to balance the number of new runners and veteran runners participating evenly. In addition, the committee likes to have 20 countries represented as well as 20 to 25 states in the United States.

The entry committee also looks at all aspects of a person, similar to what they might do with someone applying for a job. People who are involved in charity work

AN EXCLUSIVE CLUB

Completing the Badwater 135 is one of the rarest athletic achievements in the world. Fewer than 1,000 people have completed the race in its history. By comparison, more than 6,000 people have climbed the world's tallest mountain, Mount Everest.

People come from all over the world to run the Badwater 135. Tetsuo Kiso and Hiroyuki Nishimura are both from Japan.

or have helped the running community in some way can stand out among their peers. An appreciation and respect for the race is also a plus. People can show this with their answers to some of the interview questions such as "What does 'Badwater' mean to you?" or "Which Badwater 135 veteran do you admire the most and why?"

Ultramarathoner Rhys Jenkins of Wales first applied for the Badwater in 2016. He had completed the three longest races in the United Kingdom. He also works with a running charity and for a company that organizes ultramarathons worldwide. Still, he had to wait four years to get in.

Even when someone is accepted, the race isn't free. Each entrant in the 2023 race paid $1,595. And the entry doesn't include expenses such as the athlete's travel costs, supplies, and support crews. But to the athletes, it's a small price to pay to compete in the world's toughest footrace.

TRAINING

The list of accepted athletes traditionally comes out in February, five months before the July race. Fourteen-time Badwater finisher Arthur Webb says that sauna training was one of the secrets to his success. After doing his daily run—Webb ran 120 miles (193 km) a week for three months—he spent an hour in a 170-degree-Fahrenheit

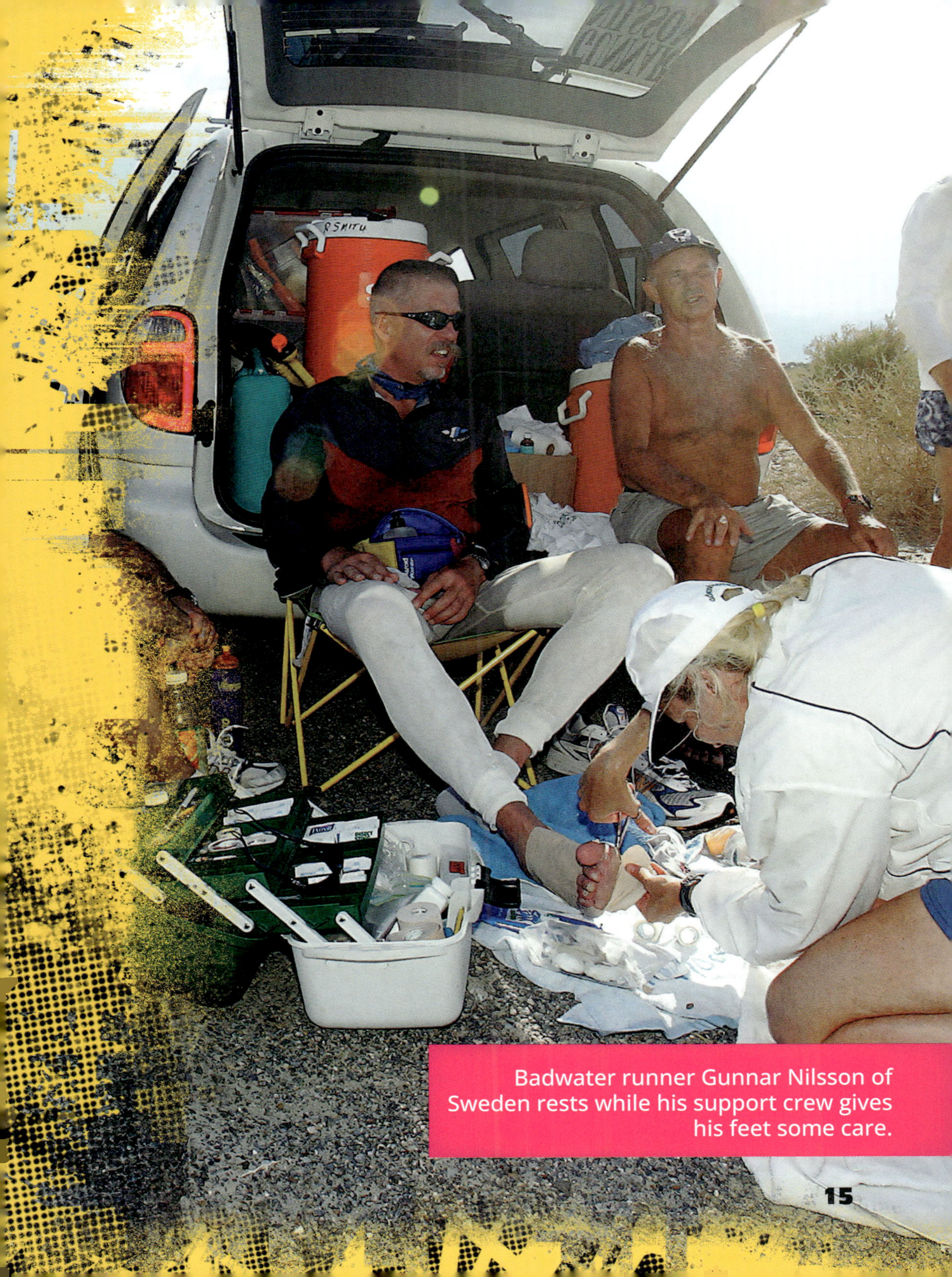

Badwater runner Gunnar Nilsson of Sweden rests while his support crew gives his feet some care.

(76.7°C) sauna. The sauna not only helps the runner prepare for the heat, but also helps the body prepare to process the huge amounts of liquid that a runner needs to consume during the race in order to stay hydrated.

Not all athletes may have regular access to a sauna. But they can get a similar effect by going for a run in a full sweatsuit. Webb sometimes even made his commute home from work with the heat on high in his car. However it's done, heat training is a must.

The heat causes a number of issues for athletes. Running 135 miles (217 km) is hard enough on the feet, but moisture from sweat causes blisters to form even more easily. Foot care is a huge part of success in the Badwater. Wearing properly fitting shoes, taping areas of rubbing, and keeping toenails short are common secrets to success.

Shoes may fit correctly at the start of the race. However, then the heat and constant impact cause feet to swell. Some athletes bring shoes that are a size larger to change into. Others cut the toe areas out of their shoes. Webb even ran a few miles in flip-flops just to get some relief.

There are no stops along the trail for water, supplies, or other services. What aid the runners receive comes from their support crews. The crew drives alongside the runner in a van or recreational vehicle. Planning out the right crew is important. Crew members don't merely hand out water and ice. Many individuals are elite athletes themselves and help pace the athlete by running alongside them.

For a first-time competitor, it helps to become familiar with the route. Since the course never changes and is run mostly on roads, some athletes have used online maps to view the entire course. Every little bit of preparation helps when tackling a race like the Badwater.

POUNDING THE PAVEMENT

Even for some of the world's toughest athletes, the Badwater 135 is a dangerous race. The heat and distance challenge even the most experienced runners. The difference between finishing and serious injury can come down to a single mistake.

Dehydration is one of the biggest threats athletes face. The human body can process only about 32 ounces (946 mL) of liquid per hour. Athletes must stay hydrated without overdoing it.

The types of liquids runners drink are important too. The body can be properly hydrated but low in electrolytes, which help regulate bodily functions. This condition can lead to painful cramping, and the athlete may need medication.

Chris Moon, who is a double amputee, runs in the 2013 edition of the Badwater 135.

Dean Karnazes, *right*, grimaces in pain as he runs the final stretch up Mount Whitney to finish the 2013 Badwater 135.

Nutrition is almost as important as hydration. Runners are often working too hard to have much of an appetite. But they still need to eat, even if they don't feel like it. As they run, they are losing 400 to 600 calories per hour. Those calories must be replaced.

Too much water and not enough food can lead to hyponatremia. Runners lose a lot of sodium, or salt, when they sweat. In the condition of hyponatremia, the body's blood sodium levels are too low. The only way to replenish them is by eating. In severe cases, hyponatremia can lead to death.

With these risk factors, it is important for runners to take the time for proper care. There is no limit on how often or for how long they stop for breaks to rest, eat, and drink. However, athletes must meet certain landmarks on the course within an allotted amount of time, since they have 48 hours total to complete the entire race.

OVERCOMING CHALLENGES

Dean Karnazes has seen just about everything the Badwater 135 has to offer, especially the heat. The 10-time finisher has seen eggs fry on the hot pavement. As Rhys Jenkins found out in 2019, that level of heat can cause foot swelling. The pain was so bad he could barely stand. Blisters can also become so painful that athletes have had to be carried off the course.

Racers must be mentally strong too. The physical
exertion and lack of sleep can cause the mind to play tricks
on a runner while on the course. Karnazes once imagined
he was seeing dinosaurs out in the desert.

The race is so long that runners can get discouraged.
That is where a support crew can also come in handy.

Michael Wardian, a 2011 Badwater 135 competitor, takes an ice bath with the help of his support crew.

Kelaine Conochan completed the Badwater in 2021. But many times she wanted to quit, only for her crew to tell her she was just a few miles from a landmark and to keep going. It takes a team to keep the runner motivated.

CHAPTER 4

THE GREATEST REWARD

The thrill of finishing the Badwater 135 lasts a lifetime. But before a racer can enjoy the feeling, they first have to recover. Running the race affects every part of a person's body, and it can take weeks to fully recover.

By some estimates, it can take a day to recover for every hour that a race lasted. For athletes who need all 48 hours to complete the Badwater, that's 1 1/2 months of recovery time. Some effects are more temporary. Most athletes quickly heal from blisters and get back on a normal sleep schedule. But there can be long-term effects, such as joint and back pain.

Valmir Nunes of Brazil won the 2007 Badwater 135 with a record-setting time of 22 hours, 51 minutes, and 26 seconds.

Australia's Grant Maughan crosses the
finish line as a first-time competitor
in 2013.

Caryn Lubetsky of Miami Shores, Florida, finished her first Badwater 135 in 2019. While she looked forward to a shower after the grueling race, she found she couldn't physically stand long enough. She had to settle for a bath, but she struggled to lift her leg high enough to get into the tub. Nonetheless, she couldn't wait to run Badwater again.

Athletes likely aren't worried about any of the physical pain as they're crossing the finish line. For many people, the Badwater 135 is the crown jewel of their athletic careers. Its unique challenge makes the race stand out among the rest in the world of ultramarathons.

Kelaine Conochan of Washington, DC, felt just one thing when she finished the Badwater—relief. She felt so glad to be done with it. But later, the meaning of her rare achievement really started to sink in. Conochan reflected the next day after finishing the race and said, "It was like I experienced the entirety of human emotion all at once. Love and pain. Terror and triumph. Anger and affection. Humble but invincible. Close to dead but never more alive. And very, very sweaty."

PRIDE OVER PRIZES

Aside from the feelings of pride and accomplishment one receives from finishing the Badwater 135, all finishers earn the same prize—a belt buckle. There is no prize money or extra reward for the winner. The buckle is considered prestigious enough, as fewer than 1,000 people on Earth have one.

Athletes traditionally celebrate their achievement together with a pizza party following the race. Then they go their separate ways. While many people attempt the Badwater just once in their lives, many others are yearly competitors. The record for most finishes belongs to Marshall Ulrich of Fort Morgan, Colorado. He finished the race 20 times between 1990 and 2015.

While sporting events like the Olympic Games favor young athletes, that isn't the case at the Badwater 135. The average age of entrants in the 2021 race was 49. The field is made up of athletes who have a lot of experience and have worked a long time to qualify for a race like the Badwater.

That includes Bob Becker of Fort Lauderdale, Florida, who became the oldest finisher in race history in 2022. The 77-year-old was so determined to finish that he did so on his hands and knees. His finish came just over the

For many runners, the feeling of crossing the finish line is such a thrill that it motivates them to come back and run the Badwater again another year.

48-hour mark, but he was awarded an honorary finish for his determination.

The Badwater 135 is known as one of the most elite ultramarathons in the world. It takes a huge physical and mental toll on all who enter it. But those who finish belong to an exclusive club for life and set an example for athletes everywhere.

GLOSSARY

basin
A geographic area lying at a lower elevation than the area surrounding it.

calorie
A unit of measure of energy in food.

contiguous
In contact, such as touching along a border.

cramping
A condition in which muscles tighten, often due to dehydration.

dehydration
A condition in which the body does not have enough water.

elevation
The distance above sea level.

elite
Among the best at something.

endurance
The quality of being able to do something for a long time.

prestigious
Having great value to others.

sauna
A small room heated by steam.

solitude
The state of being alone.

BOOKS

Gagne, Tammy. *Death Valley*. New York: AV2 by Weigl, 2019.

Hanlon, Luke. *4 Deserts Ultramarathon Series*. Minneapolis, MN: Abdo Publishing, 2024.

Sebra, Richard. *California*. Minneapolis, MN: Abdo Publishing, 2023.

ONLINE RESOURCES

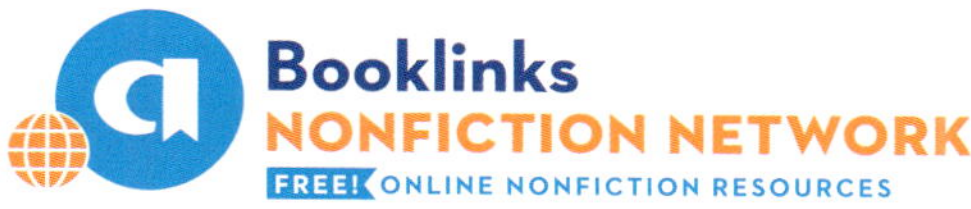

To learn more about the Badwater 135, please visit **abdobooklinks.com** or scan this QR code. These links are routinely monitored and updated to provide the most current information available.

INDEX

Badwater Basin, 8
Becker, Bob, 28

Chapman-Markle,
    Pamela, 4–7
Conochan,
    Kelaine, 23, 27

Death Valley,
    California, 4–8
Death Valley
    National Park,
    6–7
dehydration, 18

Furnace Creek,
    California, 8

hyponatremia,
    20–21

Jenkins, Rhys,
    14, 21

Karnazes, Dean,
    21–22

Las Vegas, 7
Lubetsky,
    Caryn, 27

Mount Everest, 12
Mount Whitney, 8

Olympic
    Games, 28

Ulrich,
    Marshall, 28
United
    Kingdom, 14

Wales, 14
Webb, Arthur,
    14–17

Yoshihiko,
    Ishikawa, 28

ABOUT THE AUTHOR

Anthony K. Hewson is a freelance writer originally from San Diego. He and his wife now live in the San Francisco Bay Area with their two dogs.